My Black Life Matters

BY MICHAEL A. BROWN

THIS BOOK IS DEDICATED TO...

The Voiceless.

To those who think you haven't been heard,

you have. Your life matters.

First Edition

Edited by Michele L. Mathews

Layout by Good Dharma Design, LLC

ISBN: 978-1-7356041-9-0

Library of Congress Control Number: 2020925026

Hey. Come here. Shhhh...
I'm Malik. What am I doing?

Running. Why?
I am one of the smart kids in class.

I love school.
But the other kids make fun of me. A lot.

I love learning. I sit at the front
of Mrs. O'Shaughnessy's class.

I like the way she teaches.
I like to answer questions.

I get picked on, too. At lunch.
In the halls. At the gym. In the stalls.

Dismissal can seem like a track meet.
Running like I have slave feet.
Not every day. But most days.

Why should I have to run
from those who look like me?

Shouldn't my Black life matter?
It matters to me. I'm tired of running.
Just wanna be free.
One day, someday, I hope they'll see.

Come with me, quick!
I know where we can hide.
To my friend's house.

When I run, it's close by.
She's one of the few who understands me.
The few who care.

"Hey, girl!"

"Hi, Malik! You running again?" she asked.

"Yeah," said Malik. "You know. I just *had* to outsmart Keith in class."

"Who's your friend?" asked Keisha.

"He's a new kid in our class.
We met while I was running."

Hi! Your name is...

I'm Keisha. I like to sing.
No, wait. I LOVE to sing.

My favorite song is "Lift Every Voice and Sing".

Malik helped me find my voice.

I was all alone with no one who'd listen.

I was shy for a while. Why?

I was touched by my mom's man-friend, boyfriend, something like that. I don't know who he is that well.

I came to her and told her. Wasn't anything sexual.
I just felt uncomfortable. She ignored me.

I felt alone. My house no longer a home.

Why should I be ignored
by someone who says she loves me?

Shouldn't my Black life matter?
It matters to me. Got tired of being silent.
Now I sing!
Just wanna be free.
One day, someday, I hope she'll see.

re y'all came, I was in a chat," Ke

)h, let me guess. Is it Matt?" Mali

"Yes! Come say hi, the both of y

ey, Matt. Malik's here. He brought
while running here."

guess.   again?

Hey, I'm Matt. And you are...?

Nice to meet you.
You met Malik kinda the same way we did: running.

My face? Oh, that's old.
Was bigger than that two days ago.

Well, I ran into a wall. Clumsy me.
Left my glasses at home.

So, I didn't see. That wall that had been there.
Nor that chair. Or that toy. Or that broom. Or those stairs.

It's like she doesn't even try.
Got real mad when I asked her why.

No help at home. Too many at school.
A recipe for creating fools.

Why should I be beat by someone who should teach me?
If she doesn't know, can she learn with me?

Shouldn't my Black life matter?
It matters to me. Got tired of being beat.
So, Malik and I meet!
Just wanna be free.
One day, someday, I hope she'll see.

Gasp! They all said, "It's Keith!"

"Come on out!" said Keith.

"No! You try to fight me almost every day," Malik said.

"Why? I don't bother you. I look like you. Why do you want to fight me?"

"Do you hate school? I love it!" said Malik

"I know you do," said Keith.
"That's why I chase you. I can never catch you.

You're too fast. Except this time,
another kid saw you run to this house.
So, I found you here.

"I get beat at home by my dad for getting bad grades. I even get beat when he has bad days."

"Yeah," said Keith, "because why should I get beat
by my dad with smelly feet?

Shouldn't my Black life matter?
It matters to me."

"Heeeeeey. What's funny?" Keith asked.

"You said smelly feet," said Keisha, laughing.

MASLOW'S HIERARCHY OF NEEDS

ABRAHAM HAROLD MASLOW

(April 1, 1908 - June 8, 1970) was a psychologist who studied positive human qualities and the lives of exemplary people. In 1954, Maslow created the Hierarchy of Human Needs and expressed his theories in his book, *Motivation and Personality*.

SELF-ACTUALIZATION

A person's motivation to reach his or her full potential. As shown in Maslow's Hierarchy of Needs, a person's basic needs must be met before self-actualization can be achieved.

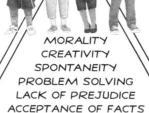

MORALITY
CREATIVITY
SPONTANEITY
PROBLEM SOLVING
LACK OF PREJUDICE
ACCEPTANCE OF FACTS

SELF-ACTUALIZATION

SELF-ESTEEM • CONFIDENCE
ACHIEVEMENT
RESPECT OF OTHERS
RESPECT BY OTHERS

ESTEEM

FRIENDSHIP • FAMILY
ASSOCIATIONS
ACTIVITIES

LOVE/BELONGING

SECURITY OF:
BODY • EMPLOYMENT • RESOURCES
MORALITY • THE FAMILY • HEALTH
PROPERTY

SAFETY

BREATHING • FOOD • WATER • SLEEP
HOMEOSTASIS • EXCRETION

PHYSIOLOGICAL

ABOUT THE AUTHOR

Born in Chicago, IL, Michael A. (Mike) Brown, MA is the author of a revolutionary social emotional children's book series, What I Tell Myself, beginning with What I Tell Myself FIRST: Children's Real-World Affirmations of Self-Esteem. Based on Maslow's Hierarchy of Needs, this book of real-world affirmations highlights the various abilities and attributes of the reader while exposing readers to realistic possibilities of rejection of difference in various forms thereby enabling readers to form mental frameworks to surmount those forms of rejection and achieve positive self-actualization. Mr. Brown continues the mission to heal and empower all with the What I Tell Myself series of books.

Mr. Brown is a product of the Chicago Public School system. He served in the United States Army and in various communities as a police officer. He is currently the President and Chief Executive Officer of MABMA Enterprises, LLC and the principal instructor of Security Training Concepts, a training agency specializing in collegiate / career occupational courses in multiple criminal justice and self-defense-related disciplines. Mr. Brown also serves as a nationally-certified anger management specialist and Crisis Prevention Institute-certified nonviolent crisis intervention instructor. He is the father of four beautiful children and believes in raising them into the best strong, capable, productive, responsible, and most importantly, happy human beings they can be. A former adjunct college professor and advocate of education, Mr. Brown is a graduate of Governors State University in University Park, Illinois, having been conferred a Bachelor of Arts degree in Interdisciplinary Studies (Criminal Justice, Psychology and Philosophy) in 2006 and a Master of Arts degree in Criminal Justice in 2012. He serves as an innovative and fresh approach to leadership, training, and empowerment and is a member of the International Law Enforcement Educators and Trainers Association, the National Anger Management Association, and the Society of Children's Book Writers and Illustrators.